DATE DUE

The Let's Talk Library™

Let's Talk About Foster Homes

Elizabeth Weitzman

The Rosen Publishing Group's
PowerKids Press™
New York

Published in 1996 by The Rosen Publishing Group, Inc.
29 East 21st Street, New York, NY 10010

First Edition

Book design: Erin McKenna

Photo credits: Cover and all other photos by Seth Dinnerman.

Weitzman, Elizabeth.
    Let's talk about foster homes / Elizabeth Weitzman. — 1st ed.
        p.   cm. — (The let's talk library)
    Includes index.
    Summary: Explains why one goes to a foster home, who foster parents are, what to do if things don't work out, and other matters regarding foster care.
    ISBN 0-8239-2310-X
    1. Foster home care—Juvenile literature. 2. Foster children—Juvenile literature. [1. Foster home care.] I. Title. II. Series.
    BF723.D3W44 1996
    155.9'37—dc20   96-3335
                                                            CIP
                                                             AC

Manufactured in the United States of America

Table of Contents

Diego

Seven-year-old Diego stood shyly behind his big sister, Ana. He had promised her he would be brave. But now that they were walking into their new home, he just felt scared.

Ana and Diego were joining a **foster family** (FOS-ter FAM-ih-lee). Their new foster mom and dad were ready and excited to welcome Diego and his sister. But Diego wasn't sure how he was going to feel about them.

◀ It can be scary to move in with a new family.

Why a Foster Home?

We all know that grown-ups usually take care of kids. But sometimes things don't work that way. Sometimes the kids have to worry about the grown-ups. Other times nobody gets taken care of at all.

If an adult can't raise a child, a foster parent may offer to help. Foster parents will take care of you until your **birth parent** (BURTH PAYR-int) can, or maybe even until you can take care of yourself.

In some families, the kids take care of the parents. This is not healthy. ▶

Who Are Foster Parents?

A foster parent can be anyone. But almost all foster parents have one thing in common: They love being parents. In fact, your foster parents probably asked for a child just like you.

Your foster parents will be different from your birth parents. They may eat foods you've never tried. They may never watch TV. Give them a chance. You'll probably like them. After all, you're there because they really want to help you.

◄ As a foster child, you may be asked to try new foods or follow new rules.

Your Birth Parents

Many kids stay in foster homes because their parents are going through hard times. These kids only stay in foster homes for a little while. When their parents are ready, the children go back to live with them.

But sometimes, children can't ever go back to live with their parents. Sometimes the parents have gone away or have died. Some parents are too sick to raise a child. No matter what, it is *never* your fault if you can't go back to live with your birth parents.

Some foster kids can't go back to live with their birth parents. ▶

Your Brothers and Sisters

If you have brothers or sisters, you might all have to live in different foster homes for a while. But just because you don't live together doesn't mean you won't see each other.

Tell your foster parents that you'd like to see your brothers and sisters as often as possible. They'll try to make sure you get to spend time together.

◀ Your foster parents want you to be happy. They will try to make sure you get to spend time with your brother or sister.

Everyone Has Different Rules

In a foster home, people you hardly know can tell you to go to bed early and eat all your vegetables. Is that fair?

It sure is.

You have to follow your foster parents' rules because you are a part of their family. If they tell you to finish your spinach or do your homework, be proud. They're doing it because they care about you.

Your foster mom takes the time to help you with your homework because she cares about you. ▶

How Do You Feel?

No matter how much your foster family cares about you, you might feel left out sometimes. After all, you've left a home you knew for one you don't. And if your new family has other kids, you might think you don't belong.

You might also be mad at your mom or dad, or feel guilty that you like your new family. Every foster child has these feelings. They're natural and normal. But you'll be even more unhappy if you keep them all inside.

◀ You may feel left out sometimes.

Talk, Talk, Talk

Whenever you feel sad or angry, there's only one thing to do. It's not shouting, or hitting, or throwing things. It's talking.

Try talking about your feelings with your foster parents. If you can't or don't feel comfortable, talk to a teacher or **caseworker** (KAYS-werker). They help kids deal with their problems every day. If you let them know what's wrong, they'll try to find a way to help you feel better.

Talk to your teacher or caseworker about how you're feeling. ▶

What If It Doesn't Work Out?

Try to get to know your foster family. Practice reading with your foster dad. Ask your foster mom if she'll help you with your homework. Remember, this family was ready to like you even before you arrived.

But even foster parents can have problems. If your foster family doesn't take care of you or hurts you at all, tell your caseworker *right away*. She'll find a better place for you to live.

◀ Try to get to know your foster family. One way to do this is to read together.

What Happens Next?

Some foster kids stay in many different homes. They may not be happy in a particular place, or their foster parents may not be able to take good care of them. Where you live does *not* depend on how special, lovable, and wonderful you are. You are all those things.

Teachers, caseworkers, and foster parents all want to make sure that you're always taken care of. They want to help you. Let them.

Glossary

birth parent (BURTH PAYR-int) Parents who gave birth to you.

caseworker (KAYS-werker) Person who finds you a foster family to live with.

foster family (FOS-ter FAM-ih-lee) Family who takes care of you when your birth parents can't.

Index